ISSUES TO INCOME

"Creating Wealth While Solving Society's Most Pressing Problems,,

---

BIANCA GOLDWELL

DESCRIPTION

Do you want to benefit financially while simultaneously changing the world for the better? Do you want to learn how to identify and address the most important social problems facing our generation? Do you want to learn about the cutting-edge approaches and business models that may assist you in making an effect and making money at the same time?

This book is for you if you indicated yes to any of these questions. This book will teach you how to:

- Recognise the link between economic and social concerns and the ways in which resolving them may benefit both you and others.
- Conduct research and analysis to pinpoint the issues that are most important to you and your target audience and comprehend the present global situation.
- Use cutting-edge approaches to issue resolution, such as social entrepreneurship, impact investment, and helpful technology, to develop solutions that can help both people and the environment.
- Create the ideal business model for your solution, and use different tools and metrics to assess the effect and profitability of the model.
- Overcome the difficulties and dangers of becoming a social entrepreneur, and take inspiration from the achievements of others who have gone before you.

This book offers a thorough introduction to social entrepreneurship for anybody interested in entering the area or learning more about it generally. You will acquire the information, abilities, and motivation need to bring about constructive change in the world by reading this book. Don't pass up this chance to become a part of the social entrepreneurship movement that is building a better future for everyone. Place your order now!

TABLE OF CONTENT

CHAPTER ONE

INTRODUCTION

What if you could use the greatest issues facing the globe to your advantage?

Imagine a society where issues like social injustice, poverty, hunger, sickness, and climate change aren't merely problems that can't be solved, but rather profitable economic possibilities. A daring future in which business people, investors, and inventors not only reap financial rewards but also significantly improve the quality of life for billions of people.

It seems too wonderful to be true, isn't it?

Yet it isn't. Currently, it is taking place all over the globe. And you may participate in it.

You'll learn in this book how to make money while addressing society's most critical issues. You'll discover how to pinpoint the markets that have the greatest promise, develop ground-breaking solutions, and expand them to serve millions of clients. Additionally, you will discover how to use relationships, technology, and social impact to leave a lasting legacy.

This Novel is definitely not for the weak of heart. It is for the daring, the imaginative, and the bold. It's for those who want to change the world and get very wealthy in the process.

Are you willing to follow them?

Then continue reading. The trip has started.

THE RELATIONSHIP BETWEEN ISSUES AND INCOME

The central focus of this book is the connection between problems and money. It is predicated on the notion that the most important issues facing our society also provide the most lucrative possibilities for business owners, investors, and inventors. They may provide value to themselves and the world by resolving these issues.

According to the book, there are four key reasons why problems might become sources of income:

- First, problems are the unfulfilled wants and aspirations of billions of people, particularly in the developing world. These individuals are prepared to pay for things that will make their life better, such having access to clean water, health care, education, and electricity.

- Second, problems give rise to new markets and sectors that are ready for innovation and disruption. These marketplaces and sectors are often ineffective, fragmented, or controlled by monopolies that do a poor job of satisfying their clientele. Entrepreneurs may dominate various marketplaces and sectors by providing superior goods and services.

- Third, different stakeholders, including governments, funders, NGOs, the media, and consumers, pay attention to and support concerns. These parties may provide entrepreneurs useful resources, such as finance, subsidies, rules, alliances, publicity, and feedback, which can help them grow their products and expand their consumer base.

- Fourth, problems have a positive societal effect that may help entrepreneurs and their products build their reputations and brands. This effect may also start a positive feedback loop that increases investor interest, staff engagement, and consumer loyalty.

These four arguments demonstrate how problems may be turned into sources of money for people who are eager to accept the task of resolving them. The book offers several case studies of successful businesspeople who have operated in a variety of industries and locales. Additionally, it offers helpful advice on how to locate, confirm, and carry out your own issue-to-income opportunity.

THE VALUE OF ADDRESSING SOCIAL ISSUES

Every society has issues that need immediate attention. Both "social issues" and "social problems" are often used within the same sentence. However, what is the definition of social issues? Why do they cause issues? And what is the root source of societal problems?

Social problems are circumstances or behaviors that have a detrimental effect on society's constituents and call for a remedy. That is, these social issues affect both individuals and big groups of people, causing disturbance or misery.

We can determine if a problem is a social concern based on four criteria:

- A sizable section of the population suffers as a result of the issue.

- The majority of the populace recognises this situation as a serious one that demands attention.

- The issue runs counter to what the bulk of the populace believes to be the ideals or tenets of that civilization.

- Through social activity, access to resources, or legislation, the problem may be resolved.

Numerous issues plague most communities. However, if the problem doesn't fit all four of the aforementioned criteria, it is not regarded as a social problem.

Let's take the issue of young adults not getting enough sleep as an example. Teachers, parents, and even teens themselves might be harmed by this problem, among other individuals. However, it is not seen as a social issue if the majority of the populace does not perceive this as a serious issue.

Social issues include concerns including poverty, racism, gender inequality, health inequalities, environmental degradation, and abuses of human rights that have a major impact on a large number of individuals in a society. Taking on social concerns may help people, organizations, and society as a whole in many different ways.

Improving people's lives is at the heart of addressing social concerns. It entails making certain that people have access to necessities like food, education, and healthcare since they are crucial for their wellbeing and personal development.

If social problems are not resolved, they may become obstacles to prosperity and economic progress. By tackling them, we may fully realise the creative and entrepreneurial potential of a diverse workforce, resulting in everyone's economic prosperity.

Societies generate stability, social cohesion, and a reduction in conflict through addressing social concerns. It's about fostering a community where individuals can work together and feel safe, eventually leading to peace and social harmony.

Taking on social concerns is a declaration of fairness and human rights. It affirms our dedication to maintaining these principles by recognising that every person deserves respect, decency, and equal opportunity regardless of background.

We build a solid basis for a sustainable future by tackling societal challenges. In order to secure a more resilient and prosperous world for future generations, we must recognise the deep connections between the health and well-being of our communities and the planet.

CHAPTER TWO

RESEARCH AND ANALYSIS FOR PROBLEM IDENTIFICATION

Any research endeavor should start with investigation and analysis to identify problems. They assist you in finding relevant literature and supporting data to back up your assertions as well as in defining the scope, objective, and direction of your study.

A particular problem or knowledge gap that you wish to fill with your study is referred to as a research problem. It could be a problem that has to be solved in the real world or it might be a theoretical issue that seeks to learn more. A research issue ought to be precise, manageable, and open to investigation.

A research question is a focused, targeted inquiry that directs your investigation into the issue. It ought to be unique, relevant, and responsive. An inquiry may be categorical, comparative, causal, or evaluative.

You may draw inspiration from a variety of sources, such as your own or your employer's experience, current literature, theory, or discussions on the subject matter, to formulate a research issue and inquiry. Additionally, you may speak with stakeholders who are knowledgeable about the issue, practitioners, or specialists.

You must do a literature review to analyze a research topic and query. This entails looking up, analyzing, and synthesizing current sources related to your subject. A survey of the literature enables you to:

Develop a theoretical framework or conceptual model for your study. Identify the present level of knowledge on the issue. Look for gaps and restrictions in past research. Situate your research within the body of existing literature.

You must use a systematic method while doing a literature review:

Define your search's focus and keywords, then use a variety of databases and search engines to locate relevant information.

- Use standards to choose and exclude sources based on their value and applicability.

- Apply critical appraisal methods to the analysis and comparison of the sources.

- Classify and summarize the sources based on topics, frameworks, or categories.

- Compose a synthesis and summary of the sources.

Problem-Solving Research Examples

Researching potential solutions is the next stage once a problem has been discovered. Here are some alternatives for doing research to address possible issues or seize possibilities discovered by your business:

Market segmentation to classify customers based on shared characteristics or purchasing behaviors: You may segment your market with the use of research, then create adverts that target just those particular clientele. To fully comprehend your market groups, you must gather both qualitative and quantitative data.

Promotional Research to Assess Advertising Strategies' Efficacy: While increasing earnings is crucial, it's also prudent to avoid money waste, particularly when it can be avoided with a little effort and investigation. If your business uses adverts, there are several things to think about and keep an eye on. You might easily be overpaying in the wrong places if you aren't optimizing your advertising budget to make sure your advertisements are successfully maintaining and attracting clients.

Distribution study to get products to the right retailers: This kind of research helps identify the best locations to sell a company's products and the best ways to deliver them to those locations. Planning the best route to get your goods from the producer to the retail shelf requires this crucial stage. Additionally, it assists in deciding where your goods will be kept in addition to helping you choose which shops to partner with.

Pricing Analysis to Find the Best Product Prices: Setting the pricing for your goods is one of the most crucial marketing procedures. Maintaining the customer's perspective while being faithful to your company's primary objective of maximizing earnings requires a careful balance. Will decreasing your rates result in more customers? Would raising prices to maximize profit be preferable? How accommodating are your clients to even modest price increases? These are just a few of the issues that need to be taken into account, which is why understanding how consumers respond to price sensitivity is crucial.

In order to successfully compete in the market, you need to think about doing secondary research or seeing how your goods are utilized. Product research is used to test new or revised items or to complete test marketing. A strategy to find new goods or find ways to improve current ones is by testing various components. One example of this is updating a product to compete with newer ones.

IDENTIFYING PRESSING ISSUES

A critical first step in every social or political undertaking is identifying the most urgent problems. Pressing problems are those that have a large social impact and call for quick solutions. Poverty, climate change, racial discrimination, and access to healthcare are a few examples of urgent challenges.

Determine which topics are urgent by:

- Specify the parameters and goals of your project. What is the primary purpose or aim of your project? Who are the project's intended audience or beneficiaries? What results or effects are you hoping your project will have?

- Analyze your position. What are the circumstances and trends that are now affecting your project? What are the SWOT analysis of your project's strengths, weaknesses, opportunities, and threats? What are your stakeholders' requirements, interests, and expectations?

- Draw inspiration and information from a variety of sources. To learn more about the issues affecting your society, you may utilize data, statistics, reports, surveys, interviews, focus groups, observations, or media. To come up with ideas for prospective problems, you may also draw on your personal or professional experience, as well as on current literature, theory, or discussions.

- Assess and rank the problems. The relevance, urgency, severity, feasibility, and solvability of any problem may be evaluated using these criteria, as well as their significance and viability. To visualize and contrast the difficulties, you may also utilize tools like problem trees, problem matrices, or issue maps.

- Create an issue statement. A problem statement is a succinct and unambiguous summary of the problem that your project will try to solve. The primary issue, its origins, consequences, breadth, and size should all be included.

There are several important problems in the world that need immediate attention and resolution. Among the most prevalent and harmful ones are:

- Coronavirus: The global health, social, and economic effects of the COVID-19 pandemic are unparalleled. As of September 20211, it has sickened over 230 million individuals and killed about 4.7 million. Additionally, it has interfered with human rights, commerce, education, travel, and livelihoods. The pandemic response has been inconsistent and insufficient globally, including problems like unequal access to vaccines, false information, and variations. Additionally, the epidemic has made pre-existing issues like poverty, inequality, and climate change worse.

- Unemployment: Due to the epidemic, millions of individuals have lost their jobs and source of income. According to the International Labour Organisation, there were 255 million fewer full-time jobs available on the global labor market in 2020, or 8.8% fewer working hours. Global labor income fell by 8.3% as a consequence, or $3.7 trillion2. Retail, tourism, the hotel industry, and the entertainment industry are the most impacted. Women, young people, migrants, and undocumented employees are among the most vulnerable workers. The state of the labor market is unknown and is dependent on how the epidemic develops as well as the political decisions made by governments.

- Poverty and social inequality: Prior to the pandemic, these issues were pervasive and long-lasting issues in many nations. The World Bank estimates that in 2017, 689 million people lived in severe poverty (earning less than $1.90 per day3). In 2020, an additional 97 million people are anticipated to be living in severe poverty as a result of the pandemic3. In addition, the epidemic has expanded wealth disparities inside and across nations. According to the World Economic Forum, the pandemic may undo years of progress made in lowering inequality and lead to a "great divergence" in the global population.

- Climate change: One of the gravest existential dangers to both people and the earth is climate change. It results from human activities like burning fossil fuels, deforestation, and agriculture, which build up greenhouse gasses in the atmosphere. Millions of people's weather patterns, ecosystems, biodiversity, food security, water supplies, health, and sense of security are already being impacted by climate change. The average world temperature has increased by around 1.1°C since the pre-industrial era, and if present emissions continue, it is expected to reach 1.5°C by 2030. This is according to the Intergovernmental Panel on Climate Change (IPCC). The effects on life on Earth would be severe and permanent.

- Financial/political corruption: In many nations, financial/political corruption harms democracy, governance, development, and human rights. The misuse of authority, whether it be public or private, is known as corruption. It may manifest itself in a number of ways, including bribery, theft, fraud, cronyism, nepotism, money laundering, and illegal financial flows. Corruption undermines public faith in institutions, squanders public funds, skews markets, stokes conflict, and impedes societal advancement. More than two-thirds of the nations in the world, according to Transparency International, have a Corruption Perceptions Index (CPI) score below 50, which is considered to be very high.

These are only a few of the urgent problems that the whole globe is facing and that need our attention and action. Numerous other concerns, including crime and violence, gender equality, human rights, education, health, migration, and peace, are equally crucial and connected to these ones. To successfully solve these concerns, we must collaborate at all levels—local, national, regional, and global—and take an all-encompassing, inclusive, and sustainable strategy. To support our choices and actions, we must also rely on accurate information, proof, and statistics.

UNDERSTANDING CURRENT SOCIAL ISSUES IN THE WORLD

Current social issues in a society are those that affect a large number of individuals on a broad basis and need collaborative effort to resolve. Some of the current social issues affecting the world include health, the environment, the economy, politics, human rights, and culture. Due to their frequent complexity, interdependence, and dynamic nature, these issues provide significant challenges for individuals, groups of people, and governments.

To understand the current social difficulties facing the world, you need do certain steps, such as:

- Select the topic that intrigues or concerns you. An issue that directly affects you, a bigger population, or the environment are all options. You may choose an issue that affects people locally, nationally, or internationally. For example, you could be interested in local homelessness or climate change on a worldwide scale.

- Research the issue using a range of data and analytical sources. You may utilise data, studies, surveys, articles, books, podcasts, videos, and more to learn more about the facts, causes, affects, and solutions of the issue. To examine the issue from a variety of angles, you may also use a variety of frameworks and perspectives, such as historical, sociological, psychological, ethical, or global. For instance, you may use Bing's online search function to get relevant and reliable information across a variety of websites. You may also use Bing's question answering capability to get answers to specific questions about the issue.

- Evaluate and put your newly learned information to use. You must assess the relevance and veracity of the information you have obtained, as well as contrast and compare information from different sources and viewpoints. You should also group, summarize, and identify the main points of the information you have learned. You may use tools like notes, outlines, summaries, or diagrams to help you with this step.

- Speak out and let others know your opinion on the circumstances. You may use a range of communication and media techniques to express your opinion on the subject, inform others of it, and persuade them of it. You may use different forms of artistic expression and creative media to illustrate the issue or your suggested remedy. You may, for instance, talk about the issue in a speech, letter, blog post, or article. You might also create a piece of visual art that depicts the issue or your suggested fix.

Art is a powerful instrument for drawing attention to social issues due to its capacity to do it in a distinctive and captivating way that encapsulates complicated and emotive notions. Art may expose misconceptions, promote compassion and solidarity, and inspire people to take action. There are several ways to use art to draw attention to social issues, such as:

- Create a piece of visual art that depicts the problem and how it impacts people or the environment. There are many other visual art forms you may use, such as painting, drawing, collage, sculpture, photography, and video. You may also use alternative materials, such natural or recycled goods, to convey your message. For example, you might create a painting that shows how air pollution impacts people's health or a sculpture that uses plastic waste to highlight the issue of ocean pollution.

- Write a poem, a story, an essay, or a song outlining your perspective on the issue and how it affects you or others. You are free to use a number of styles and techniques while writing, such as poetry, metaphor, dialogue, and comedy. You may also use a range of genres and techniques, such as satire, rap, and non-fiction. Write a poem that criticizes prejudice and injustice, for example, or a short story that describes the situation of immigrants and refugees.

- Stage a play, dance performance, comedy show, or musical that illustrates the issue, its causes, and possible solutions. There are several performance art elements that you may use, such as clothing, accessories, music, and movement. Additionally, there are many other methods to express oneself, such as via realism, symbolism, irony, or satire. For example, you may present a dance that celebrates the diversity and persistence of indigenous cultures or stage a play that raises awareness of domestic violence and its detrimental impact on women and children.

- Create a campaign, a festival, a workshop, or an exhibit to showcase your artwork and invite people to come and learn more about the issue. Public parks, cultural institutions like museums, online platforms like social media, and open spaces like online platforms are just a few sites where you may exhibit your artwork. You may use a range of strategies and tools, such as interactive activities (like quizzes), educational materials (like leaflets), or calls to action (like petitions), to engage your audience. For instance, you may conduct a workshop where participants learn how to create their own art project on the subject, or you might arrange an exhibition that displays your visual art work and provides details and resources for resolving the issue.

These are just a few examples of the ways in which you may utilize art to draw attention to social issues. You may also combine other creative and media methods to produce a project with more impact and depth.

CHAPTER THREE

INNOVATIVE PROBLEM-SOLVING TECHNIQUES

What comes to mind when you think of the concept of innovation? We often conceive of it as a result—a finished product that, owing to "out of the box" thinking, towers above that of a rival. But innovation is more than that. It encompasses the complete process of developing new methods to provide improved procedures, goods, and services.

Finding a new path might be challenging since every breakthrough initiative necessitates a detour from the standard. It might be challenging to break free from our habitual thinking patterns since we have a tendency to do so. Cognitive distortions like catastrophizing or confirmation bias may make it difficult for us to understand the subtleties of a situation, leading us to believe the issue "can't" be resolved.

The good news is, we can utilise a team dynamic to cultivate abilities that encourage creative problem-solving. To begin with, though, we must recognise the obstacles that can stand in the way of such advancement and consider the limitations we have placed on addressing problems.

If you're feeling stuck, take into account these inquiries:

Have you made an effort to create the channels of communication required to create and preserve the interpersonal connections that foster innovation? It's crucial that everyone on the team feels at ease sharing their thoughts while working as a unit. Innovation does not emerge out of thin air. It necessitates a discussion of various approaches to framing and attacking problems. Think of it as a game of numbers: the more options you have, the more likely you are to discover an effective answer. The success of the initiative is also more personal to those who feel heard.

Which risks are you personally exposed to? Working with individuals who can recommend taking a measured risk might translate to intrapreneurial success if you are a risk-averse person, and vice versa. The most effective leaders combine several viewpoints and blend them into a solution.

Do you consider and accept reasonable recommendations? Or do you reject potentially workable solutions because they are flawed? Sometimes we have to live with some ambiguity or uncertainty since a solution may not fully resolve every facet of a situation.

Are preconceived notions about how things "should" be done preventing you from developing new ideas? Old methods are not necessarily the best, and something that formerly held up under inspection may not do so now. Breaking such cognitive habits requires acknowledging how past solutions' limitations restrict our ability to solve problems creatively.

Ways of Addressing Issues

You may use the techniques or procedures listed below to discover original and useful answers to challenging challenges. They may support creativity and progress in your professional or personal life as well as assist you in overcoming obstacles and adjusting to change.

Brainstorming is a strategy that entails coming up with as many ideas as you can in a short amount of time without critiquing or assessing them. You may discover novel solutions, get your creative juices flowing, and explore other viewpoints.

Six Thinking Hats is a method that encourages using several "hats" or roles to examine a topic from many perspectives. For instance, the red hat represents sentiments and emotions, the black hat represents risks and disadvantages, the yellow hat represents opportunities and rewards, the green hat represents creativity and options, and the blue hat represents procedure and control. You may make better judgments with this strategy by avoiding biases, taking into account various factors, and so on.

Challenge your understanding of the rules: This strategy entails questioning the presumptions and constraints that keep you from coming up with a solution. You may extend your horizons, find new chances, and liberate yourself from traditional thinking with its assistance.

Fresh Eyes: This method entails approaching a subject as if it were the first time you've ever seen it or enlisting the help of a stranger to provide their perspective. You may discover fresh approaches, prevent tunnel vision, and obtain new insights thanks to it.

Pose the "dumb" inquiries: Let rid of your expert ego and try approaching the issue as if you were starting from scratch. What glaring problems are there on the ground level? To recognise fresh chances, you sometimes need to let go of restricting information. The fact that innovation involves learning is a basic part of it.

Utilize your prior experiences: You have a history of learned information that may be useful in unexpected ways. You could discover the answer to a present issue in an unrelated but insightful lesson from your history.

Testing your solution against possible flaws, hazards, and objections is known as "bullet proofing." It may aid well in problem - solving, problem- anticipation, and confidence-building.

IMPACT INVESTING

The term "impact investing" describes financial commitments "made into businesses, organizations, and funds with the purpose to achieve a demonstrable, positive social or environmental effect alongside a financial return. Impact investing is fundamentally about matching an investor's values and views with the allocation of funds to deal with social and/or environmental challenges.

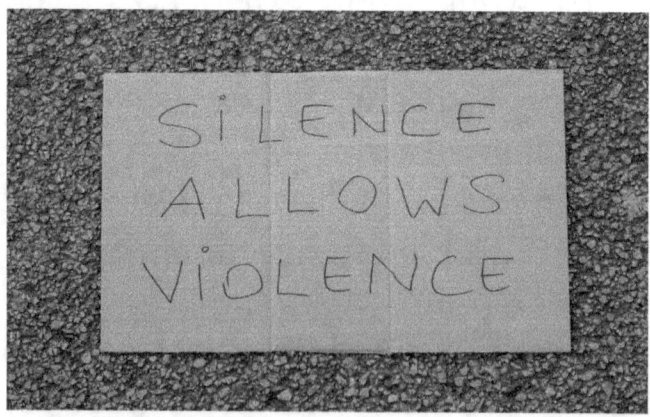

With the new instrument of impact investment, you may tackle social problems and earn money or profits at the same time. Effect investing is the practice of making financial investments in businesses or initiatives that also provide a beneficial social or environmental effect. By doing this, you may advance important causes like financial inclusion, renewable energy, health care, and education while also profiting from your investment.

You must do some preparation and study if you want to utilize impact investing as an innovative strategy.

- Define your values and objectives. What type of effects do you wish to have on society or the environment? What type of financial gain are you anticipating? What level of risk are you ready to accept? How long are you prepared to wait for the return on your investment?

- Look for appropriate opportunities. Various asset types, such as stock, debt, or fixed income, provide impact investment potential. Additionally, you may choose from a variety of industries, including microfinance, healthcare, education, and agriculture. To identify and contrast various possibilities, you might utilize internet platforms, networks, or brokers. You may also seek the advice of professionals or consultants who can assist you in assessing the possible effects and financial performance of various investments.

- Put money into it. You may make your investment after choosing a chance that aligns with your objectives and beliefs. You could be required to sign a contract, pay a fee, or provide some collateral, depending on the kind of investment. Additionally, you may need to abide by any legal or regulatory standards.

- Track and assess your effect. You should monitor and evaluate your investment's effects and financial performance after you make it. To gauge the social or environmental effects of your investment, you may use a variety of instruments and frameworks, such as Impact Reporting and Investment Standards (IRIS) 1 or the Global Impact Investing Rating System (GIIRS) 2. The internal rate of return (IRR) and net present value (NPV) are two examples of common financial metrics that you may use to calculate the return on your investment.

- Sell all of your stock. You may take your money out of the investment whenever it achieves maturity or the exit point. You could get a one-time payment, a series of payments, or a percentage of the earnings, depending on the investment type. Additionally, you may be able to reinvest your funds in yet another impact investment opportunity.

Investors have a variety of impact investing opportunities, and they may decide whether to invest in established or developing areas. Impact investments are made across several sectors, such as:

Energy, particularly clean and renewable energy, in the areas of healthcare and education
Agriculture

Social, Environmental, and Governance (SEG): SEG describes the actions taken by an investment that may materially affect how well it performs. By highlighting possible risks and opportunities above and beyond technical assessments, the incorporation of SEG variables improves conventional financial research. While social conscience is present, financial success is still the primary goal of SEG value.

Socially responsible investing: This goes beyond SEG by deliberately excluding or choosing assets in accordance with predetermined ethical standards. There may be a religious, moral, or political motivation at work. Responsible investing employs SEG elements to impose negative or positive screening on the investment universe, as opposed to SEG analysis which determines values.

Following are some instances of impact investment in various industries and areas:

- Purchasing shares in a technological firm that seeks to create more effective methods for treating and purifying water.

- Investing in mortgage-backed securities with the intention of funding low-income communities' access to affordable housing.

- Making an investment in a social company like d.light that manufactures and distributes solar lights and other sustainable energy products in underdeveloped nations.

- Contributing to a fund that promotes equitable finance, sustainable forestry and agriculture, waste and water management, renewable energy, and these other areas.

- Making an investment in a microfinance organization that offers low-income business owners, particularly women, loans and other financial services.

POSITIVE TECHNOLOGY

Positive technology is a cutting-edge instrument that may assist you in resolving social challenges while generating cash or profit. The scientific and practical approach to employing technology to enhance the quality of the human experience is known as positive technology. It is founded on the ideas of positive psychology, which is the academic study of healthy human development.

Below are some examples of ways to use helpful technology as a tool for creativity:

- Making and marketing products that support happiness, mental health, and general well-being. For instance, you may develop a tool that tracks and improves users' mood, sleep, or stress levels, or an app that encourages users to practise mindfulness, gratitude, or positive affirmations.

- Building and providing online communities, platforms, and services that encourage social interaction. You might, for instance, develop a platform that links individuals with comparable interests, ambitions, or principles, or a service that makes it easier to engage in online volunteering, coaching, or mentoring.

- Creating and providing online training materials or programmes that provide users information or skills that may enhance their personal or professional life. For instance, you may create a programme that teaches users how to launch and build a social company or a course that teaches users how to deal with anxiety, despair, or trauma.

By employing positive technology as an inventive tool, you may produce income and profit for yourself by collecting fees, subscriptions, or commissions for your goods or services, as well as create value for your clients and society by raising their quality of life. You may also be able to draw in investors who are enthusiastic about funding ventures that benefit society or the environment.

Risks associated with using positive technology as an innovative tool are:

- Security and privacy concerns. Biometric, behavioral, and emotional data are just a few examples of the kind of personal data that positive technology often collects and analyses. This information may be sensitive and open to abuse, hacking, or unauthorized access. Positive technology users should be aware of the providers' and platforms' data protection rules and practices and take precautions to protect their security and privacy.

- Moral and ethical conundrums. Positive technology may bring up moral and ethical issues, such as who should determine what is best for the user, how to strike a balance between the user's autonomy and well-being, and how to prevent manipulation or coercion. Users of beneficial technology should be aware of the objectives, processes, and results of the technology they use and have the option to change their choices or opt out.

- Adverse or unanticipated effects. Positive technological advancements may have unanticipated negative effects, such as the development of reliance, addiction, or solitude. Users of positive technology should be aware of any risks or adverse effects and seek professional assistance if they feel any discomfort or impairment.

SOCIAL ENTREPRENEURSHIP

The word "social entrepreneurship" refers to the practice of employing corporate tactics and expertise to solve social, cultural, or environmental issues. People who explore novel approaches with the potential to improve society are known as social entrepreneurs. They often mix financial objectives with social or environmental purposes, and they assess their performance based on both monetary and social results. Here are some instances of social entrepreneurship:

- Grameen Bank: This microfinance organization offers loans and other financial services to low-income individuals in rural Bangladesh and other countries, particularly women. Muhammad Yunus, the organization's founder, received the Nobel Peace Prize in 2006 for his efforts to fight poverty and advance women's rights via social entrepreneurship.

- D.light: This social venture manufactures and distributes solar lights and other green energy items in underdeveloped nations. Its goal is to offer millions of people without access to power with dependable, inexpensive, and clean energy. Additionally, it generates employment and revenue prospects for regional business owners who sell its goods.

- Coursera: This is an online learning environment that provides courses and programmes from renowned institutions all over the globe. Its mission is to make high-quality education and lifelong learning available to everyone, wherever. In order to address the skills gap and the demands for workforce development in many sectors, it also collaborates with governments, organizations, and businesses.

- TOMS: This is an additional example of social entrepreneurship that modified its business strategy when necessary.

The one-for-one concept, which many socially conscious companies subsequently imitated, gained popularity in 2006 thanks to TOMS. The business would give away a pair of shoes for each pair of shoes sold.

They sold a product to customers who could afford it, supporting their capacity to operate a profitable company, and by supplying new shoes to underserved neighborhoods, they were able to make a real difference in the lives of those in those neighborhoods. Over time, however, researchers came to the conclusion that just giving away shoes wasn't leading to long-lasting change, and it could even have harmed communities if the contributions were upsetting nearby shoe shops.

Over time, TOMS modified their donating model a few times in response. They now set aside a percentage of their earnings for grassroots products, collaborating with neighborhood organizations, and giving financial contributions to assist long-lasting change.

From TOMS' experience, other firms have gained knowledge. For instance, Warby Parker's one-for-one programme provides eye tests and reasonably priced eyewear for those in need for every pair of eyeglasses sold.

Benefits

The word "social entrepreneurship" refers to the practice of employing corporate tactics and expertise to solve social, cultural, or environmental issues. People who explore novel approaches with the potential to improve society are known as social entrepreneurs. They often mix financial objectives with social or environmental purposes, and they assess their performance based on both monetary and social results. The following are some advantages of social entrepreneurship:

- It may provide a motivating answer to issues that many people face, particularly the underprivileged or marginalized populations. Social entrepreneurs may come up with innovative and practical methods to enhance other people's quality of life by using their creativity, enthusiasm, and capacity for taking calculated risks.

- You may work for yourself and live by your own principles. It is possible for social entrepreneurs to operate with greater autonomy and independence so they may follow their own instincts and ambitions. They might also take pleasure in the fulfilment that comes from working on worthwhile projects.

- It may generate revenue and employment for both you and others. By making money off of their goods or services and providing job and income possibilities for those who share their mission or profit from their solution, social entrepreneurs may help the economy.

- It enables you to locate your own goods or services in line with your hobbies and passions. Social entrepreneurs may select from a wide range of industries and professions, such as education, health, energy, agriculture, finance, etc., that can solve various social or environmental challenges. Additionally, they may tailor the design and delivery of their goods and services to their target audience and clientele.

- Both society and the environment may benefit from it. By resolving some of the most important problems that impact a lot of people, social entrepreneurs may improve local communities and the global community. They might encourage others to support their cause or emulate them.

Risks

The practice of social entrepreneurship has various hazards. Among the dangers that social entrepreneurs could experience are:

- Obtaining funds: Lenders may be hesitant to invest in companies that do not have obvious or substantial profit margins, therefore social entrepreneurs may have trouble securing funding for their ventures. For grants, contributions, or subsidies, social entrepreneurs may have to compete with other for-profit or nonprofit organizations.

- Backlash: Those who disagree with social entrepreneurs' causes, cast doubt on their intentions, or criticize their strategies may meet with opposition, criticism, or animosity. Legal, political, or cultural obstacles that restrict their effect or endanger their safety are other issues that social entrepreneurs could have to cope with.

- Ethical and moral conundrums: When making choices that have an impact on their stakeholders, clients, beneficiaries, or the environment, social entrepreneurs may experience ethical and moral conundrums. Social entrepreneurs may need to strike a compromise between their own ideals and principles and other people's needs and expectations. They may also need to refrain from using pressure, coercion, or exploitation on the individuals they are there to help.

- Unintended or unfavorable effects: Social entrepreneurs may have unfavorable or unforseen effects on society or the environment. These effects could include dependency, addiction, or social isolation among their beneficiaries, as well as the displacement or disruption of existing markets or systems.

How To Become A Successful Social Entrepreneur

To become a social entrepreneur, you need to have a passion for fixing a social, cultural, or environmental issue, and a feasible company plan that can bring good impact and financial benefits. You also need to take certain practical actions to make your concept become reality. These are some measures that you may take to become a social entrepreneur:

- Write a mission statement. This is a quick overview of what you want to accomplish, how you want to do it, who you want to serve, and what value you want to deliver. A concise mission statement may help you clarify your purpose, objectives, and target market.

- Research the field. This entails understanding more about the issue you wish to tackle, the current solutions and competitors, the prospective consumers and beneficiaries, and the possibilities and obstacles in the industry. You may utilise internet platforms, networks, or middlemen to identify and evaluate alternative choices.

- Make a business strategy. This is a document that defines your company model, strategy, operations, finances, and impact measurement. A strong business plan will help you evaluate your assumptions, identify your strengths and shortcomings, and explain your vision to others.

- Find financing. This entails acquiring the resources you need to start and build your firm, such as money, equipment, or talent. You might seek for numerous sources of money, such as grants, contributions, loans, equity, or income.

- Launch your company. This comprises setting up your legal structure, registering your company name and logo, collecting the appropriate licenses and permissions, and developing your website and social media profiles. You also need to sell your goods or services, create connections with your consumers and partners, and deliver on your commitments.

- Measure your influence. This entails measuring and analyzing the social or environmental impacts of your organization, as well as the financial performance. You may use several techniques and frameworks to quantify your effects.

CHAPTER FOUR

BUILDING THE RIGHT BUSINESS MODEL

A business model is a company's blueprint for producing a profit. It outlines what goods or services the firm delivers, who are its consumers, how it reaches and serves them, and how it makes income and controls expenses. A business model also represents the beliefs and aims of the organisation, and how it expects to produce value for its stakeholders, such as investors, workers, suppliers, and society.

Types of Business Model

There are many different kinds of business models, which vary according to the market, industry, and corporate strategy. Typical illustrations include:

- Retailer: A retailer deals directly with customers to offer products or services. It may function offline, online, or both. It may focus on a certain market or provide a range of goods. Walmart, Amazon, and Starbucks are among examples.

- Manufacturer: A manufacturer creates products from components or raw materials. It has the option of selling its goods to other companies (B2B) or to consumers (B2C). Additionally, it may contract out all or a portion of its manufacturing operations to other businesses. Nike, Apple, Toyota, etc.

- Subscription: Customers pay a regular price to a subscription firm in order to access its goods or services. Depending on the features, advantages, or length of the membership, it may provide many plans or tiers. Additionally, it may mix subscription with other sources of income like sales or advertising. Examples include Dollar Shave Club, Netflix, and Spotify.

- Freemium: A freemium firm provides a free introductory version of its product or service and charges for further, more advanced capabilities. It may utilise the free users as a marketing channel to draw in paying clients or as a source of information or feedback. For instance, Dropbox, LinkedIn, and Skype.

Build It Right

A corporation must consider not just its financial success, but also its social and environmental effect while developing a sustainable business strategy. A sustainable business strategy seeks to produce long-term value for all stakeholders by addressing society's and the planet's demands and difficulties. The following are some stages to developing a sustainable company model:

- Determine your value proposition: What is the one-of-a-kind advantage or solution that your product or service offers to your customers? How does it assist them in resolving a problem or meeting a need? What distinguishes it from your competitors?

- Establish your target market: Who are your ideal clients? What are their traits, interests, behaviours, and aches and pains? How large is the market opportunity? How can you successfully reach and serve them?

- Evaluate your environmental and social impact: What are the positive and negative environmental and social impacts of your company activities? How can you reduce your environmental impact while increasing your social contribution? What are the dangers and possibilities that come with your influence?

- Select your revenue model: How will you profit from your product or service? What are your pricing and costing strategies? How will you strike a balance between profitability and affordability? What metrics will you use to assess your financial performance?

- Align your values and goals: What are the fundamental concepts and values that influence your company choices and actions? What are your long-term objectives and vision for the future? What methods will you use to convey and demonstrate them to your stakeholders?

- Validate your assumptions and hypotheses about your product or service, customers, market, impact, and revenue by testing and refining your business model. How are you going to get input and data from your stakeholders? How will you apply them to your company model?

Establish It Right

A corporation must properly define and convey its business model in order to build it. A business model canvas (BMC), which is a visual depiction of the essential components of a business model on one page, is an effective tool for this purpose. A BMC may aid a business in:

- Describe and prioritize its value proposition;

- Summarise and deconstruct its business strategy.

- Examine its advantages and disadvantages.

- Share its approach with its stakeholders

- Test out various possibilities and scenarios

Although there are other BMCs accessible online, they typically have the following components:

- Value proposition: The distinct advantage or remedy that the item or service offers to consumers.

Customer segments are the categories of clients that the business services or plans to serve.

- Channels: The methods through which a business contacts and provides its clients with goods or services.

- Customer relationships: The kinds of interactions that the business creates and keeps up with its clients.

- Revenue streams: The ways in which the business receives money from selling goods or providing services.
The resources that the business requires to develop and provide its goods or services.

- Key activities: The primary duties that the firm carries out in order to produce and provide its goods or services.

- Important alliances: The group of partners and allies who assist the business in developing and delivering its goods and services.

- Cost structure: The significant expenditures the firm makes to produce and provide its goods or services

MEASURING IMPACT AND PROFITABILITY

You must determine the relevant indicators that indicate the favorable and unfavorable impacts of your company operations on society and the environment if you want to assess the social and environmental impact of your enterprise. You could wish to track your carbon emissions, water use, trash production, customer loyalty, employee happiness, community involvement, or social innovation, for instance. Utilizing a variety of methods and frameworks, such as the Impact Reporting and Investment Standards (IRIS) 1 or the Global Impact Investing Rating System (GIIRS), you must also gather and analyze data on these variables. You may compare your effects to those of others or benchmarks, quantify and evaluate them, and communicate your impacts to your stakeholders with the use of these tools.

The social and environmental effect of a firm is quite complex. Take Tesla, for example, which produces electric automobiles that substantially cut emissions over the course of their lifetimes but is under fire for its hiring procedures. The firm could get good grades from an impact-investing approach, but it ranks poorly from a SEG one, with neither paradigm fully reflecting the situation. As a consequence, both strategies are making people more frustrated: Elon Musk, the CEO of Tesla, has called the S&P 500 SEG Index's removal from the index "an awful swindle," and other major asset managers have changed the names and tone of their impact funds in response to criticism of impact investing.

Profitability

You must compute the gap between your revenue and costs to evaluate your company's profitability. Revenue is the money you make by offering your goods or services for sale. The expenditures you pay to produce and distribute your goods or services—such as those for materials, labor, rent, utilities, taxes, etc.—are referred to as expenses. To determine profit, use the following formula:

Profit = Sales - Expenses.

You may also figure out your profit margin, which is the portion of income that you retain in profit. To determine profit margin, use the following formula:

(Profit / Revenue) x 100 equals profit margin

A bigger profit margin indicates that you are more adept at controlling expenses and producing revenue. You may monitor and calculate your income, costs, profit, and profit margin using accounting software or internet resources. To summarize and report your profitability, you may also utilize financial statements like the income statement.

CHECKING THE SUM-UP OF CHALLENGES

Businesses that pursue both financial and beneficial social and environmental outcomes are known as impact-driven initiatives. Finding funds, assessing effect, expanding, and adjusting to changing circumstances are just a few of the difficulties and difficulties they must overcome. Here are some strategies for overcoming these challenges and adjusting to a changing environment:

- Obtaining funding: Impact-driven enterprises may have trouble attracting investors who are ready to back both their profitability and their purpose and vision. Impact-driven businesses may find alternate financing sources like grants, contributions, crowdsourcing, or impact bonds to get around this problem. Additionally, they may establish connections with other impact-driven business owners, groups, or platforms that might introduce them to possible donors who share their objectives and beliefs.

- Measuring effect: In addition to their financial success, impact-driven initiatives must show how their actions have a positive social or environmental impact. effect-driven businesses may address this issue by using a variety of tools and frameworks, like the Impact Reporting and Investment Standards (IRIS) or the Global Impact Investing Rating System (GIIRS), to quantify and disclose their effect. They may compare their effects to those of others or benchmarks, quantify and evaluate them, and communicate their results to their stakeholders with the use of these tools.

- Scaling up: In order to have a greater effect and make more money, impact-driven businesses must increase their influence and reach. Impact-driven businesses may scale up their solutions through using partnerships, creativity, and technology to address this issue. To reach new clients, recipients, or markets, they might employ digital platforms, tools, or services. To improve their effectiveness, efficiency, or distinction, they might innovate their business models, processes, or products. They may also collaborate with other players who can aid in their development, such as allies, mentors, distributors, and suppliers.

- Adjusting properly to changing circumstances: The Impact-driven businesses must adapt to the shifting demands and expectations of their clients, beneficiaries, stakeholders, and the environment. Impact-driven businesses might develop an adaptable and agile mentality and business strategy to overcome this obstacle. They are able to track and assess the signals and trends that have an impact on their market and industry. Additionally, they may test and experiment with many possibilities and situations to determine which one fits their condition the best. Additionally, they may adapt their methods as a result of their triumphs and mistakes.

CONCLUSION

The capacity to turn obstacles into opportunities or solutions that may provide value or income is known as the power of turning issues into income. It is a talent that may assist businesspeople, inventors, and agents of social change in making gains and having a good influence.

Finding a market or societal need that is not being satisfied by current goods or services is one approach to transform problems into money. The next step is to create goods or services that can fit the identified need. For instance, the social company d.light manufactures and distributes solar lights and other renewable energy items in underdeveloped nations where millions of people live without access to electricity. By resolving this problem, d.light not only enhances the lives of its clients and beneficiaries but also makes money from sales.

Utilising technology, creativity, and partnerships to scale up or enhance current solutions is another approach to convert problems into money. An online platform like Coursera, for instance, provides courses and programmes from prestigious institutions and organizations all around the globe. Digital technology enables Coursera to reach more students, expand its menu of options, and save expenses. Coursera can also address the skills gap and workforce development needs in various sectors by collaborating with governments, nonprofits, and businesses.

Measuring and communicating the social and environmental effect of your actions in addition to your financial success is a third strategy to convert problems into profits. By doing this, you may draw in additional clients, financiers, and associates who concur with your ideals and objectives.

Your Duty to Make the World Better

You have a duty to do good deeds in the world as an entrepreneur who profits from other people's difficulties by utilizing your abilities, assets, and influence. Here are a few options on how to go about doing that:

- Practice ethical and open business principles. Avoid taking advantage of, misleading, or hurting your clients, staff, suppliers, rival businesses, or the environment. Observe the rules and legislation that are relevant to your profession and locality. Be truthful and responsible for your choices and behaviors.

- For your clients and society as a whole, create value and provide solutions. Don't simply think about getting money; also think about changing the world. Offer creative, practical, and reasonably priced answers to the problems your target market is facing. In order to improve your goods or services, look for feedback and improvement prospects.

- Back social initiatives that are consistent with your goals and beliefs. You may do this by giving up a percentage of your earnings, offering your time or skills, collaborating with charities, or starting social projects inside your business. Additionally, you may utilize your platform to advocate for causes that are important to you and your neighborhood.

- Act as an example for other business owners and prospective business owners. Share your expertise, wisdom, and perceptions with others who want to follow in your footsteps or gain information from you. Mentor, coach, or counsel individuals who need direction or assistance. Encourage, inspire, and empower people to follow their aspirations and objectives.

To sum up, as a businessperson who profits from the issues of others, you have a duty to advance society via leadership, ethical behavior, and the creation of value.

Keep in mind that becoming an entrepreneur involves more than just generating revenue. All people are entrepreneurs, according to Muhammad Yunus, the Nobel Peace Prize recipient and creator of Grameen Bank. We all worked for ourselves while living in the caverns, gathering our own food. The beginning of human history was there. We repressed civilisation as it emerged. Instead, we changed because they inscribed on us, "You are laborers." We lost sight of our entrepreneurial nature.

RESOURCES

SOCIAL CAUSES

In various developing nations, you may support a variety of social causes according to your preferences, guiding principles, and interests. Poverty, inequality, corruption, war, and human rights are some of the most important concerns that these nations are now dealing with. The following are some instances of social causes that deal with these problems:

- Reducing poverty: There are organizations you may assist that are trying to raise the quality of life for the millions of Africans who are struggling to satisfy their basic requirements. These organizations could provide services including food security, livelihood possibilities, water and sanitation, education, health care, and microfinance. A coalition of more than 2,000 civil society organizations working on different elements of poverty reduction and sustainable development, for instance, is known as the (Nigeria Network of NGOs).

- Reducing inequality: You may help organizations that promote social justice and inclusion for all Africans and seek to close the wealth-poverty divide. These groups would support equitable taxes, open government finances, social protection, gender equality, and access to opportunity. For instance, you may donate to **Oxfam**, a global organization that fights extreme poverty and injustice.

- Fighting corruption, which is a significant barrier to growth and democracy, is something you can help via donations. These organizations may keep tabs on government expenditures, reveal fraud and power abuse, call for accountability and good governance, and inform people of their rights and obligations. For instance, you might donate money to (a Nation's Transparency body), which is a local affiliate of the international anti-corruption movement that publishes reports, carries out polls, and plans campaigns to address corruption problems.

- Organizations that aim to prevent and settle disputes, which are often sparked by ethnic, religious, political, or economic issues, may get your help. These groups may help warring parties communicate, mediate disputes, promote peace, find common ground, and provide humanitarian aid. As an instance, you may help (Search for Common Ground Africa), a global organization that collaborates with regional partners to change how Africans respond to conflict and violence.

- Supporting organizations that seek to defend and advance human rights, which are often violated or disregarded in Nigeria. These groups could keep records of human rights violations, assist victims with legal matters and counseling, speak out against injustice and impunity, and encourage others to take action. As an example, you may help [Amnesty International], a worldwide organization that works to promote and defend human rights.

These are just a few of the social issues that you may help. You may research and choose from a wide range of other causes according to your interests and goals. Whatever cause you choose to support, keep in mind that your donation may improve both the world and the lives of others. It is in your power to make the world a better place for everyone who lives in it, as Nelson Mandela famously remarked.

ORGANIZATIONS

There are several international organizations, each with a unique set of objectives, activities, and missions. Some of them are associated with the UN, including UNDP, the World Health Organisation, and UNICEF. Others are independent or non-governmental organizations, like Amnesty International, Action Aid, and Oxfam. Here are a few instances of global organizations and what they do:

- UNICEF: The United Nations Children's Fund aims to safeguard and advance children's and adolescents' legal rights as well as their general wellbeing. In the areas of health, nutrition, education, water and sanitation, protection, and social policy, it offers humanitarian aid as well as development support.

- WHO: This stands for the World Health Organisation, which is the United Nations system's leading and coordinating body for health. It aids various countries in tackling or easing their public health issues, such as infectious and non-communicable illnesses, maternity and child health, environmental health, improving health systems, and disaster readiness and response.

- UNDP, or United Nations Development Programme, is the main organization in charge of sustainable development. It collaborates with the government and other partners to address issues like reducing poverty, inequality, and vulnerability, advancing democratic governance, fostering peacebuilding, boosting environmental sustainability and resilience, and promoting inclusive growth and human development.

- Oxfam: This global alliance of 20 organizations fights together against injustice and poverty in African nations. Saving lives in crises, fostering food security and livelihoods, advancing gender justice, and advocating policy change and accountability are its four main thematic areas of concentration.

Action Aid is a global federation of 45 country offices dedicated to eradicating poverty and injustice. It works with underprivileged and marginalized groups to give them the capacity to assert their rights, confront violence and corruption, have access to high-quality public services, and take part in democratic processes.

- Amnesty International: This worldwide organization of more than 10 million people works to ensure that everyone has access to human rights. It keeps track of and records abuses of human rights such extrajudicial executions, torture, arbitrary imprisonment, forced disappearances, sexual assault, and discrimination.

These are but a few of the world organizations. Depending on your interests and objectives, there are many more that you may investigate and learn from. Additionally, you may help them out by contributing, offering your time, or supporting their initiatives.

BOOK RECOMMENDATIONS

- **Captivating Wealth** by James Roland (Available on Amazon): Learn how to invest wisely, earn passively, and multiply your income. This book will show you how to overcome the obstacles that block your wealth potential and guide you towards practical steps that lead to lasting success.

- **The Millionaire Next Door**: The Surprising Secrets of America's Wealthy by Thomas J. Stanley and William D. Danko. This book reveals the common habits and characteristics of millionaires based on extensive research. It challenges the stereotypes and myths about wealth and shows how anyone can achieve financial success with the right mindset and behavior.

- **Rich Dad Poor Dad**: What the Rich Teach Their Kids About Money That the Poor and Middle Class Do Not! by Robert T. Kiyosaki. This book is a personal finance classic that teaches the difference between working for money and having money work for you. It explains the concepts of assets, liabilities, cash flow, and financial literacy through the contrasting stories of two fathers: one rich and one poor.

- **The Richest Man in Babylon** by George S. Clason. This book is a timeless parable that illustrates the principles of wealth creation and preservation. It tells the story of Arkad, a man who became the richest man in Babylon by following simple rules of money management, such as paying yourself first, living within your means, investing wisely, and diversifying your income.

- **Think and Grow Rich** by Napoleon Hill. This book is a result of a 20-year research project on the secrets of success of over 500 self-made millionaires. It reveals the 13 steps to riches that anyone can apply to achieve their goals and dreams. It also emphasizes the importance of having a positive mental attitude, a definite purpose, and a mastermind group.

- It's All About The Income: How To Make Money In Any Market by Michael Lynch. This book is a guide for investors who want to generate consistent and reliable income from their investments. It explains how to use various strategies, such as dividend stocks, bonds, real estate, annuities, and options, to create a diversified portfolio that can withstand market fluctuations and provide passive income.

TOOLS AND FRAMEWORKS FOR SOCIAL ENTREPRENEURS

Social entrepreneurs utilize a variety of frameworks and tools to help them plan, start, and expand their businesses. Here are some frameworks and tools you may find helpful:

- Business Model Canvas (BMC): This straightforward, one-page tool aids in the creation of an original business model for your social enterprise. There are nine components that make up this framework, and they address the important facets of your value proposition, customers, channels, income streams, cost structure, key resources, key activities, key partnerships, and social effect. This tool may help you express your concept to others, test your assumptions, and sketch out the business model you now have or would want to have.

- Lean Strategy Canvas: This BMC offshoot adds a possible consumer feedback loop for ongoing concept or product development to satisfy the demands of the market. There are eight components that make up this framework: the issue, the proposed solution, the most important metrics, the special selling point, the unfair competitive advantage, the channels, the client groups, and the cost/revenue structure. You may use this tool to verify the problem-solution fit, product-market fit, and business model fit of your ideas.

- Design Thinking Process: This is a methodical, logical way for dealing with and resolving issues that have several answers. Empathize, define, ideate, prototype, and test are the five steps that make up this process. Using this method, you may outline the issue you're trying to address, identify and assess potential solutions, create and test prototypes, and refine your approach in response to user input.

The Four Lenses Strategic Framework evaluates four strategic areas: stakeholder engagement, resource mobilization, knowledge development, and culture management. It is a framework for creating social companies. By interacting with your stakeholders, mobilizing your resources, expanding your knowledge base, and overseeing your organizational culture, you may utilize this framework to solve a social issue and provide lasting social impact.

Copyright